The Whole Human Race!

Come along with Mei-Xiu, Tadd, Anandani, Jack, Viviana, Chai, Pax and Zula
as they discover what we all have in common with each other!

To A.J.— the city kid who nurtures a country garden
with patience and love.

ISBN: 978-0-9847079-0-4

© 2011 Timothy S. McFadden
The Whole Human Race
www.wholehumanrace.com

Published by McFadden Creative Group, l.l.c.
Contact: publisher@mcfaddencreativegroup.com
Book Contact: info@wholehumanrace.com

This book is dedicated with love
to my mother,
Cindy Haynes McFadden,
who gave me my first breath
and a life worth breathing deeply,
my first words
and the strength to carry them,
and my first dreams
and an abundance of love
to nurture them.

You are beautiful mom, I love you!

The Whole Human Race

The world that we live in is a very big place.
So big it can hold The Whole Human Race!

Each person seems different
so different it's true,
There's no one like me
and there's no one like you.

But let's take a close look
and see what we find
when we look at
what makes up
all humankind...

1

Lips!

These lips smile.
These lips frown.
Their corners go up.
Their corners go down.

2

They whistle and sing they yell and they shout!
If you listen they'll tell you what they're all about.

These lips kiss children and parents
and grandparents too!
It's a symbol of love when agreed on by two.

Some lips have sung anthems,
cried for freedom — it's true!

Other lips in some way
may have spoken for you.

They are thick down to thin
but their shape doesn't matter
it's how you use them to make your life
and other lives better!

4

So where do you find them?
Why, let me tell you the place!
They are part of what's beautiful about...

The Whole Human Race!

Voice!

This is a voice
it's one thing you can't see
but it makes up the sounds
that help you understand me!

A voice can huff, a voice can groan,
a voice can harrumph when it feels left alone.

A voice can welcome you
or give you reason to leave,
it's a thing that has power
you had better believe!

Say hello out loud
and see how it sounds.
If you hear someone say it,
it will turn you around!

A voice can move millions of people
to pray,
or sing one tiny baby's
little troubles away.

A voice can teach you things of the past,
or fill you with lessons
of things that will last.

It can ask for love,
it can cry for peace,
you can hear when it's desperate,
you can hear when it needs.

You can change many things
with your very own voice,
but the noise that you make
is your very own choice.

Some voices are high,
some voices are low,
but it's not the sound of the voice
it's how you use it to grow.

So where do you find it?
Why, let me tell you the place!
The sound comes from inside of...

The Whole Human Race!

9

Hands

This hand has four fingers and one single thumb.
We use it for things that we do, and we've done.

A hand can hold tight
to mom or to dad,
or pull us close with a hug
when we feel kind of sad.

A hand waves hello, a hand waves goodbye.
Two hands clapped together means a happy reply!

A hand can write letters
with a pen to a friend,
or shake hands with a nation
to make troubles end.

A hand can reach out to another in need,
and bring them up to a place
where they're proud and they're free.

A hand can feel softness,
a hand can feel rough.
A hand can speak clearly
with a sign or a touch.

A hand can be short,
a hand can be long,
but it's not the way that they look
it's how you help others along.

Like a dad yelling "dinner,"
or a mom "time for school,"
or the sound of the ice cream truck
that makes your mouth drool.

Ears can hear many sounds,
like a voice singing songs.
And it reminds your own voice
how to sing right along.

They can listen to people
who just need to talk,
and at the same time
hear the birds on a walk.
Or hear people talk
on their walk in the park,
or even the songs
of a swallow or lark!

These ears can hear speeches,
or car tire screeches,
or waves hitting beaches,
or wherever sound reaches!

If these ears listen closely they'll hear many sounds,
like the noise in the forest when a leaf hits the ground.
That sound is quite peaceful — at least I have found!

An ear can hear car horns and keep us from harm,
or get us quickly to safety during a fire alarm.
It really doesn't matter
the shape of the two,
it's how you listen to others
who are speaking to you.

And where might they be? Why, I tell you right here,
on both sides in the middle of your head my dear!

If you listen to me, you'll know the place.
They hear all that's beautiful about...

The Whole Human Race!

Eyes!

These two things are called eyes,
but that you already knew.
They come in hundreds of shades
of green, gray, **brown** and blue!

18

They see so many things
but sometimes they forget
that the sunshine and stars
are the best things yet.

Some eyes have seen pain,
and almost all of them will,
but it's the caring eyes of others
that always help heal.

Some people have eyes
that may never see.
Their sight comes from within
and it's as clear as can be.

Eyes can do many things
to show how you feel,
like squint when you're angry
when you get a raw deal.
Or sparkle when you're happy
eating your favorite meal!

Remember, if the eyes that are looking
always look for the brighter,
you'll find no other eyes
looking back like a fighter.

Some eyes are thin, some eyes are wide
but it's not the shape that's important
it's what they see down inside.

So where do you find them,
these eyes that I've said?
Why, right in the middle
of anyone's head!

So go ahead,
just look on anyone's face.
See another part
that's beautiful about...

The Whole
Human
Race!

So the message you find
in the story I've told
is brighter and richer
than a zillion sacks of gold!

But you'll only be richer if you truly see
others aren't that different from you and me,
at least nothing that important.
Don't you agree?

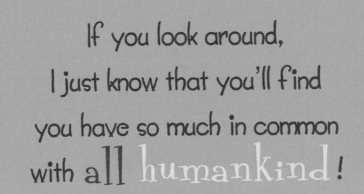

If you look around,
I just know that you'll find
you have so much in common
with all humankind!

Remember, it's not the color, or religion,
or the way people speak.
It's not how they live, or who they love,
or if their bones creak.

It's the way that they feel,
it's what comes from inside,
and it's the way that you respect them
that gives you your pride.

For each smile that you give

For each voice that you greet

For each ear that you lend

For each eye that you meet

And every hand you extend

again and again...

If you do it with goodness
and sincerity and grace...
Then YOU become a big part of what's beautiful about...

The Whole
Human Race !

— About the Book —

Here's a few things that are good to know and also a few questions.

One of the kid's in this book looks like a real-life girl who has read The Whole Human Race.
Go to the website — www.wholehumanrace.com — and you'll find a picture of her.

The dog on page five is named "Seven" and the cat is named "Chabby." What would you name the pelican?

A LARK is an American songbird. A lark with a yellow chest is called a meadowlark.
LARK is also a word that means "a carefree adventure," or "a harmless prank."
How many meadow larks can you find in this book?

In the HANDS section of the book, the line "shake hands with a nation to make troubles end," was inspired by the peace treaty between Egypt and Israel made in 1979.

The line in the book "A hand can reach out to another in need and bring them up to a place where they're proud and they're free," was inspired by Martin Luther King, Jr.

What do you think this sentence on page 19 means? "Some eyes have seen pain and almost all of them will, but it's the caring eyes of others that always help heal."

ZILLION is a word that means "a very large number."

PRIDE is a word that means many things. On page 25 it means "happiness because you did a good thing for someone else."

The word RESPECT, on page 25, means that you "treat people the way you like to be treated."

The word SINCERITY, on page 27, means "honesty." What do you think the word GRACE means?

© 2011 Timothy S. McFadden
The Whole Human Race

Published by McFadden Creative Group, l.l.c.
Contact: publisher@mcfaddencreativegroup.com
Book Contact: info@wholehumanrace.com

— About the Author —

 Tim McFadden is an author and an artist. He has been writing and creating artwork since he was a young boy.

He writes children's books, screenplays, fiction and non-fiction novels, lyrics and poetry.

He is a painter and a sculptor, and he designs furniture.

He believes that we are all creative and that we are all inspired.
He believes that we are all created equal.
He believes that we are all here to help each other experience how wonderful life is.
He believes that the common bonds of human beings can make the world a better, more peaceful place.
He believes in the sun, even when it isn't shining.
And, he believes in love.

The Whole Human Race
is first in a series of three books.

The Whole Human Race

A Quite Special Place

Your Very Own Space

Special thanks to:
Kelly Smith & Chloe Smith for editing, enthusiasm
and final approval.
Julie Sussman Perez for editing and enthusiasm.

ONE
WORLD
LOVE
PEACE

Made in the USA
Middletown, DE
24 January 2019